THE SECRETS OF A GREAT HAIRAPIST

*Lessons I've Learned
Along the Way*

By: Kim Constantineau

THE SECRETS OF A GREAT HAIRAPIST

*Lessons I've Learned
Along the Way*

By: Kim Constantineau

Copyright © 2023 by Kim Constantineau

All rights reserved. No part of this publication may be reproduced, distributed, or transmitted in any form or by any means, or stored in a database or retrieval system, without the prior written permission of the publisher.

Printed in the United States of America.

Table of Contents

Hairapist Defined [2]

A Collection of Cautionary
(Funny, Somewhat Scary) Tales [4]

Failing Forward [38]

Mindset [40]

The Psychology of Hairdressing [59]

Notes on Professional Development [71]

Bonus Affirmations [94]

Bonus Mirror Work [99]

About Me [102]

A Note to Hairstylists [105]

This book was inspired by my many years of experience as a hairstylist, photographer, therapist, social media professional, marketing chemist, artist, and friend.

In today's society, everything has changed. You need to know so much more than just hair to become a great hairstylist. You're going to go through many ups and downs to become a master at hair.
I call it ...

FAILING FORWARD.

Hairapist

hair-uh-pist: (n) A scissor wielding, miracle working, creative genius who touches more hearts than hair.

They're kind of a big deal.

HAIR IS UNIVERSAL

Yes,
Hairstylists do
much more than just HAIR!

A COLLECTION OF CAUTIONARY (FUNNY, SOMEWHAT SCARY) TALES

YOU DON'T HAVE TO LEARN YOUR LESSONS THE HARD WAY

To illustrate the need for constant professional development, I'll tell you a few tragic/comic stories about the mistakes I made as a rookie hairdresser.

**When I didn't know ...
what I didn't know!**

A TALE ABOUT SINEAD O'CONNOR HAIR

Once, one of my amazing clients brought her sister into the salon. She had jet black hair -- straight out of a do-it-yourself box. She was a natural blonde and dyed her hair black. Now, **she wanted to be a platinum blonde and** "with no brassiness."

This was a hairdresser's nightmare!

Because box dye has high ammonia content in it, it's hell to lift out of the hair. With all the ignorance of youth, I thought, "That's easy! I **can make her a platinum blonde, no problem."**

I put her hair in an old-fashioned cap with little round holes on it and pulled every hair I could through them. Then I applied the strongest bleach with 40 volume.

Keep in mind ...
It was 1988. They didn't have all the conditioners and bond building systems inside the lighteners back then.

WHEN USING HARSH LIGHTENERS, DON'T PUT THEM UNDER A HEATER DRYER

I should have told the client that it would be impossible to maintain her hair's integrity. I should have told her that at best, she would probably need about three or four appointments because it would be a process.

What I should have communicated was that I wasn't
"Wonder Woman!"

Sure, I can make some wishes come true -- just not impossible ones!
But that's my mature brain (with all my experience) talking right now.

Back then, I decided to use BW2 +40 volume, thinking
I needed power to get the black out!

I put her under a heated dryer with the cap on.
Yikesssssss!

I didn't realize it, but I was
setting her up for disaster.

It was like I put her in a brick oven.
NOT GOOD!

After 30 minutes under the dryer, her hair was bright orange! So, I washed it out, thinking -- Ok, I need to put more bleach and 40 volume on it and put her back under the dryer again for another 20 to 30 minutes. The integrity of the hair was still good.

In any case...
I wasn't too concerned about the integrity of her hair. All I was worried about was getting the orange out!!!

After 20 more minutes, her hair was bright yellow-orange! Since this was actually an improvement, I put her under the dryer for 10 more minutes to try to get all the orange out.

**When she was done, the orange was gone, but now her hair was
neon yellow!**

I wouldn't dare put her under the dryer with more bleach, so I brought her to the sink.
As soon as I touched her hair, it started falling out!!! I stared in disbelief. I couldn't breathe!!!
I was gasping for air, thinking --
What in the world do I tell her?
I was sweating, scared out of my wits. Well, you can just imagine what happened next ...
Yes, all of her hair had burnt off!!! It pulled off like when you pull a piece of cotton candy off to eat it. IT WAS A NIGHTMARE!!!

Ultimately, we had to give her a Sinead O'Connor hairdo. Thankfully, for us both, she had a similar style two years before, so it just looked like she was going back to her previous hairstyle. Somehow, she was better than I was.

**I cried for days and had nightmares for weeks. I wanted to give up
doing hair.**

Of course, after a disaster like that, you go from the top of the world, thinking you're great, to the depths of hell.

**Boy, did I feel like
the biggest failure!**

The Moral of the Story:

That was over 30 years ago.
And I can tell you that
I failed forward.

I had to learn to forgive myself. I had been arrogant. I thought I knew it all and I didn't.

So, I stopped crying and learned from my mistakes. I knew what NOT to do ever again!

This failure, in particular, pushed me to take ownership of my future success.
Because of it, I was able to teach, train, and coach others more effectively in hair and products over the next 25 years and become the master professional I am today.

A TALE OF TWO EARS

When you're young, you think you know it all. So, after I graduated high school and did really well in cosmetology school, I guess you could say I was a little full of myself.

Actually, I knew it ALL!

I felt like a SUPERHERO!!! I was *Wonder Woman*, Samantha from *Bewitched*, and Jeannie from *I Dream of Jeannie*, all rolled into one. I could twitch my nose, wave my magic wand, and do everything my client wanted!

Just as I convinced myself I could do no wrong, I realized that making mistakes was essential for my growth. In fact, I made a ton of them! You might be asking yourself right now, how bad could it be? Well, I will tell you so you can **decide. How bad would you say it is to cut the tips of two people's ears off???**

In my youth-inspired arrogance, I didn't think about pulling the ear down (big mistake) and just tried to cut the hair around it. Suddenly, there was a weird feeling when I pressed down on my scissors.

That weird feeling?

Yup, a thick piece of ear skin!!

The Moral of the Story:

If you are a beginning hairdresser, make sure you always pull down the ear before you cut around it. Don't even chance it until you have enough experience and are steady and stable with scissors!

Needless to say, the young boy and older woman never came back to me.

But just to let you know, I haven't cut anyone else's ears off in the last 20 years, so you can trust me now!

THE PERSON IN THE ARENA

"It is not the critic who counts; nor the person who points out how the strong man stumbles or where the doer of deeds could have done them better. The credit belongs to the person who is actually in the arena, whose face is marred by color and sweat and tears; who strives valiantly; who errs, who comes short again and again, because there is no effort without error and shortcoming; but who does actually strive to do the deeds; who knows great enthusiasms; the great devotions; who spends themselves in a worthy cause; who at best knows in the end the triumph of high achievement, and who at the worst, if she or he fails, at least fails while daring greatly, so that their place shall never be with those cold timid souls who neither know victory nor defeat."

-Theodore Roosevelt Revised by Coach-Kimmy

The Moral of the Story:

You NEVER want to allow someone else to bring you down emotionally with their criticism.

Instead empower yourself for greatness.

The real lesson to be learned is that you are not perfect and you will make mistakes. It's part of the process of growing.

Through practice, you will have the ability to define who you are and what you become. The critical person only plays a part in the journey for you to get better and better at your skills.

Your mindset is what matters the most -- if you think you can, you will, if you think you can't, you won't!!!

A TALE OF CHEETAH SPOTS

One time, a beautiful woman asked if I could add golden caramel highlights in her medium-brown hair. I thought, "Of course, I can. I can do ANYTHING!" Remember, I was still thinking that I was Wonder Woman at this time. So, I mixed up some bleach and 20 volume peroxide, and put tons of foils on her hair. When I checked it 20 minutes later, she had big, white cheetah spots on the top of her head!

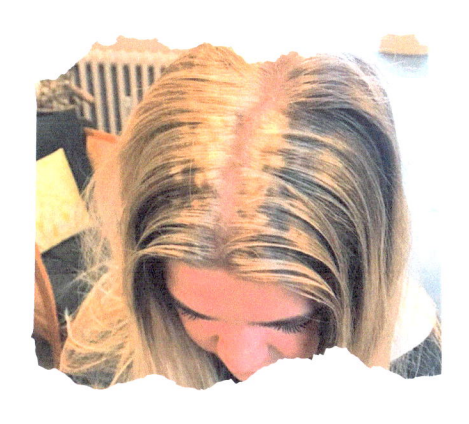

THAT POOR LADY CAME BACK THREE TIMES. I COULDN'T UNDERSTAND HOW TO GET HER HAIR LIGHT ENOUGH, REMOVE THE BRASSINESS, OR WHAT WAS CAUSING ALL THE SPOTS.

The Moral of the Story:

You never put runny bleach in a foil, on a highlight cap, or put it too close to the scalp because it swells and drips -- creating spots.

I never made that mistake again! Now, when I mix bleach to put in a foil, I mix the perfect consistency, so it will never drip and never make spots.

Vanilla Pudding is the reference for perfect consistency.

A TALE OF TWO OPINIONS

Years ago, the mother of my good friend, Lisa, was getting ready for her 80th birthday. I had stayed at her house to spend time with her and then get her ready in the morning for the big surprise party.

I worked so hard to make her hair smooth and sleek, and I was so excited because I thought she looked fabulous! She took one look in the mirror, looked directly into my eyes, and with a strong, firm voice asked,

"You really think this looks good?"

I said, "Yeah, I think it looks great!"

She didn't even look at me again
as she started redoing her hair with her little finger waves.

I was laughing so hard because I really thought it looked amazing and I could not have been more wrong!

Older women are usually very stuck in their **ways. They don't like change!**

The Moral of the Story:

What I learned is that
it doesn't matter what I like!
It only matters what someone else
likes and wants.

**We need to listen to our clients
and do what they want -- always!!!**

A TALE OF BREAKUP & BANGS

I was 15 years old, not even a real hairdresser yet, and my stepmom asked me to cut her bangs. I had been crying about a fight with my boyfriend, but told her that I would do it for her.

Before I knew it, she had no bangs at all because I cut them all off! I guess I was crying too much to really see what I was doing. And let's just say my stepmom didn't end up looking very good for quite a while.

**I thought I could do it all, no matter what my emotional state.
BOY, WAS I WRONG!!**

The Moral of the Story:

Yes, I was only 15, but **I learned that a good hairdresser has to be professional, even when they're going through a bad time personally.**

I realized that when I was upset, I could not do my best work and shouldn't even try.

A TALE OF GEOMETRY & HAIR

Once, my friend and co-worker, Jessie, and I went to Miami Beach for a five-day intense Vidal Sassoon training class.

It was a whole new world to me. It was about cutting hair with mathematics.
Wait, what???

I was terrible in math! I cried the first day in class because it was all geometry, which I hated!

It was as if hair had a whole other life -- a life I never knew even existed. It even had a new language with words like concave, convex, circle, square, triangle, interior, and exterior.

Our teacher would hold up a magazine picture and ask,

"What shape do you see in this hair? Round, square, or triangle?"

Seriously, is he kidding me?
I couldn't see any one of those shapes in the pictures!

I really wanted to knock him out! What was he talking about? After class, I got on the Internet to find out how to see these shapes and what all these new words meant.

By the third day, I ended up learning a lot. I even brought the DVDs home with me and **watched them over and over again.**

These classes fed my soul in a way that nothing else ever had.

I could escape my own turmoil and trauma and focus on the happiness I gave others through their hair.

I was finally on the receiving end of acceptance, adoration, and appreciation. I had never been there before, and I LOVED it.

REPETITION, REPETITION, REPETITION is the Mother Skill of ALL MASTERY!!!

I thought I was now an expert in this new way of cutting. Five days of intense training and watching videos at least 10 more times would make anyone an expert, right?

WRONG

So, I asked my best friend Karen to let me try it out on her. It just seemed so simple! I started cutting and cutting and cutting some more. She looked in the mirror and started **screaming at me, "OH MY GOSH, KIMMY! You chopped my hair off!"**

I was laughing so hard
I almost peed in my pants!

She was still screaming at me,
So I had to go back and angle and cut her hair the way we normally did, but it was definitely shorter than she would have liked.

She got over it,
but we never tried to give her a Vidal Sassoon haircut again!

The Moral of the Story:

This story goes back to
PRACTICE, PRACTICE, PRACTICE.

Practice makes progress, resulting in improvement and finally, perfection.

This is when Mastery is finally achieved.

Confidence comes from knowing you put the work into it!

**And hard work ALWAYS pays off!
It really is that simple!**

Two More Fact Checks

**Don't overlap a touchup and ...
Don't underlap a touchup.**

You have to go directly to the demarcation line with the new color, but if you overlap it too much, then that overlap is going to be darker than your root touchup.

If you underlap it, then you're going to have a thin gray line in between the root and the colored hair.

You must learn precision.

Eyebrow Touchups

You do not need to give people "Charlie Chaplin" eyebrows.

Take a beautiful little paint brush approach.

Take the color from the color formula to match their desired hair color to their eyebrows.

Paint their eyebrows with precision, similar to microblading or tattooing the color onto their eyebrows, creating a beautiful rich colored eyebrow.

FAILING FORWARD

It is from these awful experiences
that I learned and grew to become a
Master in my Own Skills.

My experiences helped me
to become better and gave me the ability
to help others learn and
master their own skills to become a
Great Hair Stylist.

I hope these tales make you chuckle, while reminding you about some important lessons!

You will be ...

**BETTER THAN AN AVERAGE
Hair Stylist.**

AVERAGE MEANS NEITHER GOOD NOR BAD.
IT'S IN BETWEEN.
IT'S MEDIOCRE.
IT'S STUCK IN THE MIDDLE.

**Bust out of Average and
become a
MASTER at hair.**

Some of the experiences that I have shared with you could make you want to give up. But you're not going to because you have the right mindset!

MINDSET

To me, everything we do is all about
energy, attitude, and mindset.

A few of my favorite quotes :

"**You must know yourself to grow yourself**"

-John Maxwell -

"**You must go within or you will go without**"

–Carl Jung -

"WHETHER YOU THINK YOU CAN, OR YOU THINK YOU CAN'T -- YOU'RE RIGHT!"

-Henry Ford

MINDSET

noun.

THE DRIVING FORCE IN THE QUEST FOR SUCCESS AND ACHIEVEMENT.

A MINDSET THAT COMBINES DISCIPLINE, STRENGTH, CONFIDENCE, AND AMBITION IS A POWERFUL MIND.

THIS CAN ACHIEVE ANYTHING IT SETS ITS SIGHTS ON.

A POWERFUL MIND CAN ACHIEVE ANYTHING.

HOW DID I GET HERE?

Before we really dive into mindset, I want to tell you a little more about me and my mindset that got me where I am today.

From the time I was a little girl, with red ribbons accessorizing my pigtails, I knew I would be a **hairdresser.**

In a childhood marked by trauma and abuse, getting my hair done always made me feel **good. It made me feel special.**

To me, hair meant imagination, dreams, and happiness. And later, as a teenager, with my layered locks styled to look just like Farrah Fawcett, it helped me feel like the hottest chick in town!

From the doll heads I would practice on as a child to my cosmetology classes during high school,
there was never a doubt as to what my calling would be.

My passion showed in my commitment and in my grades. I stayed after school to PRACTICE, **PRACTICE, PRACTICE** and even got straight 'A's (well, except when it came to pin curls)!

If you don't know what pin curls are, picture Shirley Temple ringlets. You roll the hair up in a tiny square, wind the hair around your finger, and put a little X bobby pin on the little curl in that square. Then you repeat that through the entire head.

My teacher was so strict that if you did one pin curl wrong out of 100, you had to do the whole set over again.

PRACTICE, PRACTICE, PRACTICE makes perfect!

Finally I got to be that 'A' student even in pin curls.

"EVEN GENIUSES CAN GET THINGS WRONG. LOOK AT EINSTEIN'S UNFORTUNATE CHOICE OF A HAIRDRESSER."
– JOSS STIRLING

Now, here I am, 51 years old at the time of writing this book.

**I am now a Salon Owner
with an
Incredible Dream Team.**

I've learned how to take my
passion for hair
and my passion for people
and marry them together to build an
awesome environment,
productive A+ team, and a
positive work culture.

Teaching, coaching, and elevating others,
is so rewarding because it transforms people
from the INSIDE OUT.

That's what I do!

Sometimes, it may seem like it is so much easier to give up, but there is something inside you that won't allow you to quit.

That comes from your mindset!

With any growing process, there are growing pains. But remember, you are resilient. You have a desire to learn and attain mastery of your hairdressing skills.

This all starts with mindset!

A shift begins to happen and on the other side of that shift, with my help, you will find **your superpowers!**

NEVER, NEVER, NEVER GIVE UP.

QUITTERS NEVER WIN AND WINNERS NEVER QUIT.

REMIND YOURSELF EVERY DAY ...

YOU ARE A WINNER!

So how do you go within to remember that YOU ARE A WINNER?

It's by getting to know yourself.

You must really learn to value yourself.

Did you ever love someone that you would do anything for them?

WELL MAKE THAT SOMEONE
YOU!

You are worthy
to be loved.

A great mantra is ...

"I am enough,
I have always been
enough, and
I will always be
ENOUGH."

This is what built my muscle of confidence.

The more I believed in myself, the stronger and more confident I became.

My confidence then gave my clients CERTAINTY and they learned to
TRUST ME EVEN MORE!

It's a LIFE CHANGER to make a difference in people's lives.

That doesn't mean it's always easy, but it always makes me happy.

People will either
inspire you
or
drain you

CHOOSE WISELY

YOUR ENVIRONMENT MATTERS

"Great people talk about ideas;

Average people talk about themselves;

Small people talk about others."

-John Maxwell

If you struggle with positivity at times, here are a few healthy reminders about how lucky and blessed hairdressing professionals are:

We get to work the hours we want.
We get to pick the days we want.
We get to choose the people we want.
We get to build the environment we want.
We get to create the culture we want.
We get to make more money than most people who work 40 hours or more a week.

We get to take charge and choose our own life.

We create our own success by realizing and appreciating all that we have.

At one point, the cycle became too much, and I felt as if I had hit rock bottom.

I was in over my head and irritated with my staff.

I had no money left and no plan.

I was stressed and lost.
I'm not going to lie, I went through hell.

If you've had this mix of emotions, I promise
YOU'RE NOT ALONE!

It is all
**within our own reach
with the right energy!**

Every good choice we make in our attitude, no matter how small,
will create great success when we choose the
positive path.

Remember:
**You can create your own vibe,
one person at a time.**

10 THINGS THAT REQUIRE ZERO TALENT

Having a positive ATTITUDE
Being coachable
Doing a little extra
Being prepared
Being on time
Making an effort
Being high energy
Being passionate
Using good body language
Having a strong work ethic

THE PSYCHOLOGY OF HAIRDRESSING

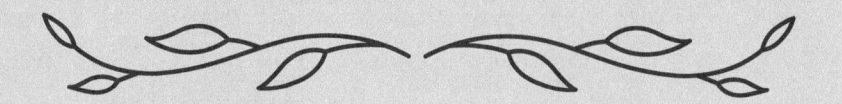

I love connecting with others, touching their lives, and in some ways, becoming a part of their families by hearing all about their great stories.

**We laugh, we cry,
we are there for each other.**

In fact, some of my clients are now my closest friends. They have helped me during tough times in my life, and I have helped them. Like I said, we are truly blessed as hair stylists.

So, what kind of atmosphere do you want to create?

Are you an energy giver or an energy drainer? Do you fill others up with goodness and positive vibes or do you give negative vibes and complain about everything?

Okay. The life of a hairapist ...

So, yes, we are a cross between a hairstylist, therapist, and psychiatrist. We are somewhat like a bartender (minus the alcohol). Everyone tells hairdressers and bartenders EVERYTHING – all their dark (sometimes dirty) little secrets, their most intimate moments, their scariest experiences, their best (and worst) of times. Trust me, when I tell you -- WE HEAR EVERYTHING! And the more they get to know us, the more they will share. It's just amazing that we hold all these secrets!

But honestly, it is one of the greatest privileges of being a hairapist. I am honored that I get to be there for my clients, who become my friends. They need someone to talk to – not to solve their problems, but just to have someone listen. That's me! That's hairstylists all over the world! You see, hair is only one part of our job.

THERAPY IS
EXPENSIVE

GET A
HAIRCUT
INSTEAD

WE'RE GREAT
LISTENERS

We become psychologists to our clients because after they trust us with their hair, they trust us with their HEARTS and SECRETS!

I have experienced this in many ways throughout my career. As hairdressers, we give our clients our undivided attention.
I have grown with my clients and in many ways, I am a part of their life stories.

I often know their whole family - husbands, wives, siblings, cousins - before I even meet them. People need friends, a support system, and connection -- and hairdressers can, and do, **provide them all.**

People who go to hairdressers often find that they want to
confess all their deepest, darkest secrets
to them.

"Once a lady was getting her hair done and began telling her stylist that she was sneaking around on her husband with a busboy from a local restaurant and they were meeting in his van."
-Stylist Autumn

Although it's interesting, it's never wise to divulge such personal details.

After all,
the hairdresser probably felt really awkward and didn't how to react or what to say!

So, why do people want to 'fess up to hairstylists anyway?

According to Psychology Today, it's partly because the client is looking in the mirror – literally – and can see the reflection of the hairdresser. It's less threatening to talk to the hairdresser in this way when compared to sitting directly opposite a therapist and staring into their eyes.

"The mirror creates the illusion of distance which makes the client feel more comfortable as he or she shares deeply personal stories."

Hairdressing means love to a lot of people.
On the surface, you can change someone's life by helping them be even more beautiful than they already are.

But even deeper than that, you can often forge **an emotional connection by being a good** listener and truly caring about them. In everyone's busy lives, their time in your chair is often their only time to unwind.

And then there are the clients who need space. And I can recognize it immediately because I've seen it all. They are going through something, and the best way for me to help is to do their hair to the best of my ability and just be quiet.

They know I'm there ... if or when they're ready to chat.

For example, when I was in my late 40s, I met a businesswoman who was extremely busy and didn't really want to speak much.

It wasn't that she was rude. She just knew what she wanted and needed at that time, and I understood and respected that. Before I knew it, by giving her the space she needed, she started opening up as I would blow dry her hair.

That simple act resulted in her becoming one of my best friends.

When Your Client Becomes Your Therapist ... and Family

I had a client named Maryellen. We were close from the beginning. In many ways, she was MY therapist because she would listen to me about my toxic childhood and offer me incredible support and kindness. I was a victim for a long time and then I became the hero of my own life. She understood me.

I began to think of both her and her daughter as my family ... and they were.

And then, the unimaginable happened ...

Maryellen was diagnosed with cancer.

I was with her every step of the way, through all the horrible treatments and sickness. I told her about juicing and brought her fruits and vegetables to try to help her get stronger.

One time, I remember saying to her that I wanted to go to her house and pray with her. She waited for me on her porch, sitting on a rocking chair wrapped in a wool blanket. It was toward the end, and we knew it. We embraced each other. We held hands and talked about her new life in heaven and what that would be like. She cried and cried -- we knew it was a moment of destiny.

She was at peace. She passed shortly after our embrace -- after our special meeting.

Another one of my lifetime clients, Nancy, was also an anchor in my life. She listened to me as much as I listened to her. I knew her hair so well and for so long that when she passed, I was the one who did her hair for her funeral. As difficult as it was, I knew it was what she would want, and I had to have faith that she was flying free with the angels. I always choose to believe in a God who loves us unconditionally.

Yes, these times are sad, but these are the moments that I am so thankful for as a hairstylist. You have a bond with your clients that is irreplaceable and invaluable. I pour my heart, mind, and soul into these relationships -- and so do they.

And people think we just do hair ...

NOTES ON PROFESSIONAL DEVELOPMENT

School is just your foundation.
When you get out of school and work in a salon, you start to get hands-on experience -- that's where the REAL magic happens! But to learn even more, you must continue to take classes, practice, and shadow someone else who has more experience. Then, confidence comes ...
"when you know you put the work into it."
-Britt Seava
Business and marketing strategist for hair stylists and host of The Thriving Stylist Podcast.

They say it takes 10,000 hours to become a pro. I believe that's true.

PRACTICE, PRACTICE, PRACTICE
results in
Progress, Improvement, and Success.

It's just that simple!

Too many people focus on self-fulfillment, but we need to focus on self-development instead.

We will only really be fulfilled (both personally and professionally) when we develop enough to be the person we are meant to be.

Self-development helps me focus on the things I'm good at, as well as the things that I can improve upon. It helps me add more value to myself and others around me.

A Lesson in Continuous Learning

Make a commitment to continue to learn – EVERY DAY!

After all, we're also learning to be chemists! We have to mix all different kinds of chemicals and understand what happens when we do.

For example, we have to know if we have well water or iron in our water, otherwise when we put highlights in hair, like lightener with volume bleach, 20 volume or 30 volume, the hair starts to smoke, especially if you put in a foil.

Who would think, right?

A NOTE ON LISTENING

Even when things don't make sense, just keep listening. One day, a couple of months or sometimes, even years later, it will all start to connect and click together like a puzzle.

Remember, sometimes things look confusing and scary, and you'll be overwhelmed. But that just means you're learning something new. This is the key to development!

Everything will begin to connect if you have patience with the process. Nothing ever REALLY good happens overnight anyway.

A Lesson in CLEAR Communication

Another great thing to remember as you develop professionally as a hairstylist is that **clear communication is VERY important!** Sometimes, clients don't get this. They'll show you a picture of a hairstyle they want that is nearly impossible (for example, we can't make someone have thicker or thinner hair).

So, it's up to you to set the record straight. Be honest with them. Tell them what will work AND WHAT WILL NOT! Don't tell them what they want to hear because they will only end up disappointed at the end.

One time, this hairdresser did a whole bunch of balayage on this young girl, who had pretty dark hair. She came running over to me about 30 minutes later and said, "Oh my God, it's bright green!"

I said, "Bright green. Well, what do you want me to do about it? Go ask the girls in the back, go look it up on Google or YouTube or something."

It's just so funny that people think hairstylists can be genie and they can just kind of blink, like "I Dream of Jeannie," and get everything they want. There's NO such thing!! Hairdressers are human and they can only do what the hair allows them to do.

After all, we may be many things, but we're not magicians ... or genies!

A Lesson in Being Organized

Another great lesson to learn as a hairstylist is to always be organized! For example, when you're mixing the same color lighteners, you have to make sure you label the 10, 20, 30, or 40 volume peroxide.

Let me say it again – LABEL all the bowls! This way, no one gets confused. Otherwise, it could be a HUGE mess!

Another important tip is that when you write your formulas in the computer, you need to put what brand you're using, the date, what colors you've used, and how much of that color you used with how much peroxide.

Be highly organized and your work will be very consistent with excellent results!

A Lesson in Honesty

I had one of my employees once tell me they did perms in school, so I trusted them. So, when I told them to put the neutralizer on, I figured they knew what they were doing. But then I realized that there was more than half the neutralizer still in the bottle!

FYI – there should not be ANY LEFT!

I had to redo the client's whole perm over again, but this all could have been avoided. It's so important to make sure that you let people know what you can and can't do. I would have simply taught her from the beginning what to do instead of being in emergency mode.

And it's not just employees you need to be careful of -- clients can embellish the truth too. I've had clients tell me they haven't done ANYTHING to their hair, and when I do something, it comes out bright neon yellow or **worse. Trust me, they did something!**

I've even had clients put henna in their hair, and there was no way it was coming out. It's crazy how it stains the hair in such a way that you can't even remove it with lightener or color. Literally, it just has to grow out.

You also have to be aware of fallacies out there (and there are a TON). Once, a scientist said when you put color on dirty hair, it won't take as well as if you wash the hair and then put the color on it. He did an experiment putting two sponges in grape juice -- a damp sponge and a dry sponge. The dry sponge went right to the tip, but the damp sponge actually absorbed and really went further to absorb so much better in the sponge.

So, there's a lot of fallacies that have been told over the years, and little white lies to be aware of.

A Lesson on Setbacks

Failures and setbacks are great tools for learning and growing and not making the same mistake again. Remember that!

A Lesson on Change

This world is always changing. It will never stop. So, we need to keep changing and keep going ... and keep growing. We all must embrace change. Things that are a little uncomfortable will always help us grow. Think of a seed when it goes into the ground and all the changes it experiences before it becomes a fruit or vegetable.

Never stop changing and growing!

SOME THINGS ARE BASIC, BUT YOUR HAIR SHOULDN'T BE ONE OF THEM!

LIVE YOUR LIFE IN COLOR

LAVISH

ISN'T IT TIME TO HAVE THE SUCCESSFUL SALON YOU'VE ALWAYS DREAMED OF?

ISN'T IT TIME TO ATTRACT THE RIGHT PEOPLE INTO YOUR BUSINESS AND LIFE?

ISN'T IT TIME FOR MORE PROFESSIONALISM, TEAMWORK, COLLABORATION, CLARITY, PROFIT, AND PEACE OF MIND?

ISN'T IT TIME TO TAKE YOUR PIECE OF THE BILLION-DOLLAR SALON INDUSTRY?

YES, IT IS! AND THE TIME IS NOW! SO, LET'S GET STARTED!

I believe my journey was for a reason.

It was to share the lessons I learned the hard way with other salon owners and managers. By going through what I did, I learned what it really takes to
**Own and Operate a
SUCCESSFUL SALON.**

So, I've built an easy-to-use system
with that knowledge and experience for YOU!

I share the shortcuts to running a salon more effectively and efficiently with the goal of making your journey a lot less painful than mine was.

With greater vision and purpose,
you WILL have the well-balanced, profitable, fulfilling salon you've always envisioned.

Whether you are an
aspiring salon owner or a salon veteran
with many years of experience,
Simple Salon Solutions provides
valuable information
to avoid mistakes and improve processes and profitability.

The Simple Salon Solutions Handbook was
designed to help you with each piece of
Salon Ownership.

It's divided into the following overall categories:

Employee Guidelines

Policies

Job Descriptions

Professional Development

Client Relations

Throughout the Handbook you will find:

Forms to create your own Salon Manual

&

The 9 Secrets for Success

Simple Salon Solutions is the
Roadmap and Foundation
to help you save resources, money, and even your sanity at times.

How fast you get there is entirely
up to you --
you can crawl, jog, run, or fly your way to all of the success you've ever imagined.

The choice is yours.
Remember, I'll give you the map, but
you're always the Driver of Your Own Life.

COMING SOON ...

Tragic Beginnings to Fairytale Endings -- Dreams Do Come True

My life story.
A story that will take the reader on a journey from tragedy to success and from toxicity to triumph.

It's raw.
It's unapologetic.
It's me.

"YOU DON'T HAVE TO BE A MOVIE STAR FOR ME TO DO YOUR HAIR,

WHEN YOU SIT IN MY CHAIR YOU'RE MY MOVIE STAR."

– VINCENT ROPPATTE

Bonus

It doesn't matter what's against you when you know what's within you.

Bonus Affirmations

TO SELF LOVE AND SELF CARE ❤
THE GREATEST PERSON BESIDES GOD TO KNOW IS ... YOU!

I AM HARD WORKING I AM INSPIRING I AM INTELLIGENT I AM IMPECCABLE WITH MY WORD I AM KIND I AM LIKABLE I AM LOVING I AM LOVABLE I AM MARVELOUSLY MADE	I AM OUTSTANDING I AM PERFECT IN GOD'S EYES I AM POWERFUL I AM RELATABLE I AM SIMPLE SIMPLE SIMPLE I AM TERRIFIC I AM UNIQUE I AM VICTORIOUS I AM A WINNER I AM YAYYYYYYYY I AM EXUBERANT

Bonus Affirmations

TO SELF LOVE AND SELF CARE ❤
THE GREATEST PERSON BESIDES GOD TO KNOW IS ... YOU!

I AM ABUNDANT I AM BRAVE I AM BRILLIANT I AM CONFIDENT I AM CURIOUS I AM DETERMINED I AM DYNAMIC	I AM AN ENCOURAGER I AM FABULOUS I AM GOD'S HIGHEST FORM OF CREATION I AM GREAT I AM GENEROUS I AM GENUINE I AM A GENIUS

Bonus Affirmations

I am highly organized, disciplined, and easy going.

I don't sweat the small stuff.

I let go of anything and everything that doesn't serve me, such as toxic people, my own toxic thoughts, or other people's toxic words.

I stay connected to healthy, happy, and emotionally whole people.

"My friends are golden links in the chain of my good."
- Florence Scovel Shinn

Bonus Affirmations Abundance

I am so Happy and Grateful now for my abundant, unspeakably joyful LIFE.

I live my life with positive thoughts and a healthy mind.

Miracles and wonders come to me every single day in every single way.

I receive all the GOOD GOD wants to give me. He makes everything go in my FAVOR.

Luck, Blessings, and Riches follow me all the days of my life.

Bonus Mirror Work

I was mentored by Lisa Nicole, who taught me how to do mirror work.
And this is how it works ...

Look into the mirror and say out loud to yourself --
"I love you for .... "
(Say at least 3 nice things that you love about yourself. For example, being brave, being smart, taking responsibility for your life and outcomes).

Then visualize those things every day until they become reality.
We create our outcomes through thought and emotions.

Bonus Mirror Work

Now, if you want to go deeper, say to yourself in the mirror ...

I forgive you for ...

Then, let it all out.

Give yourself permission to make mistakes.

Bonus Mirror Work for Hairstylists

Need more guidance? Try this to start ...

I am important, special, and valuable. I am a great stylist and I have the most wonderful, generous clients. I work hard at learning my skills in hair. I have become a great Master Stylist. I am booked solid, with a nice waiting list. I work at a great salon with great team players and a wonderful environment. I am so happy and grateful now that everything goes in my favor.

ABOUT ME

I'm Kim Constantineau, also known as Coach Kimmy. I'm an Author, Consultant, and Life Coach for Hairstylists.

Trust me, after 30+ years in the salon industry, **I have seen it all, the good, the bad, and the** very ugly. It's a rollercoaster of emotions really. I

have felt excitement, elation, pride, and then frustration, anger, and disappointment.

**It's all
a
part of life**

MY PAST ... AND MY FUTURE

I graduated from Old Bridge Cosmetology School after three years. I got my first job as a professional hair designer in Manalapan. I worked there for a few years, then moved to Inner Vision Haircutters on Ernston Road for eight years. I then spent 19 years at Gerber Salon in Keyport.

I trained with incredible beauty brands in the hair industry such as Bumble And Bumble, Oribe, Ouidad Curl experts, Wella, Davines, Redken, and Goldwell. I had some of the top best training in the hair industry.

I now take my expertise, experience, and mastery and pass it on to you. My desire and goals are to always pay it forward. All my learning, education, time, energy, and effort are always for a greater good and a greater purpose in life.

I am also in the process of publishing my life story, *Tragic Beginnings to Fairytale Endings -- Dreams Do Come True*

My core belief is that whatever you give you'll get back.

To all the Hairstylists out there,

Thank YOU for choosing this book!

I hope you were able to take my life experiences and learn from them and that you Never, Never, Never give up! Persistence, perseverance, and practice will make a Great Master Stylist.

Now, I would love to hear your story!

Have you ever experienced any dark days as an assistant or hairstylist or even as a client that you would like to share with me?

Email me at *Kimmycan7@gmail.com*

Also, please feel free to write a review about what you got out of the *The Secrets of a Great Hairapist*.

-Coach-Kimmy

Let's Scale Your Life to a Place of Abundance

For more resources to grow a miracle mindset, don't forget to check out my channels.

COACH-KIMMY.COM

Modern Teckniques, Mentoring & Mastery

- CoachKimmyC
- coach-kimmy
- stylistsuccess_coachkimmy
- coachkimmy
- +1 (732) 489-1438
- kimmycan7@gmail.com
- www.coach-kimmy.com

Made in the USA
Columbia, SC
09 July 2025